Story 1:
A miraculous flower

In a remote village, there lived a little girl named Lila. She was not like other children because her heart carried an invisible burden - it seemed heavy and full of sadness that no one could see. Lila longed to be free of this burden.

One day, Lila heard a legend about a miraculous flower that grew in the deepest forests. This flower had the extraordinary power to heal people's hearts and bring joy into their lives. Lila felt that this was her chance to find the flower and free herself from her sadness.

Determined, she set off into the forest, accompanied by her faithful companion, a small fox named Rufus.

The forest was dense and mysterious, full of shady paths and unexplored trails. But Lila felt an unknown force within her, as if the prospect of a wondrous flower had breathed new life into her.

You Are An Amazing Girl:

Inspiring and Motivational Short Stories for Girls about Confidence, Friendship, Inner Strength and Self-Esteem. Brilliant Empowering Tales for Children.

Art. RAM Publishing

Table of contents

Story 1: A miraculous flower .... 1 – 4

Story 2: The Star Flight .... 5 – 8

Story 3: Song of the Ocean .... 9 – 12

Story 4: The Butterfly Garden .... 13 – 16

Story 5: Flight of the Phoenix .... 17 – 20

Story 6: The Sound of Friendship .... 21 – 25

Story 7: The Magic of Smiles .... 26 – 29

Story 8: Anna and the Shadow Dance .... 30 – 33

Story 9: Clara, the Star Warrior .... 34 – 37

Story 10: The Mystery of the Labyrinth .... 38 – 42

Story 11: Treasure of Time .... 43 – 46

Story: 12: Melody of Nature .... 47 – 50

Story 13: Lucy and the Rainbow Catcher .... 51 – 54

Story 14: Flight of the imagination .... 55 – 58

Story 15: Crystal Source .... 59 – 62

Story 16: Dream Circus.
Vanessa's test of courage .... 63 – 66

Story 17: Agnes, the brave explorer .... 67 – 70

Story 18: The colorful canvas of the
invisible artist Ella .... 71 – 74

Dear brave hearts:

In a world that sometimes seems as big as the sky and as wide as the ocean, I want you to know that you are like the brightest stars and the most precious pearls - unique, precious, and filled with infinite potential.

You are more than just little girls; you are architects of dreams, bearers of hope, and future creators of our world. Embrace the magic within you, for it will illuminate the darkest corners and inspire those around you.

Remember that every challenge is an opportunity to grow, and every obstacle is a chance to become stronger. Like a small seed that breaks through the soil and becomes a mighty tree, you have the power within you to overcome anything. Don't be afraid to make mistakes because they are stepping stones to success.

Be curious, ask questions and discover the wonders of the world with your eyes wide open. Your imagination is a powerful force - let it unfold and let your creativity paint the canvas of your dreams.

Surround yourself with people who will lift you up and support you. Together we can create a symphony of power and unity that resonates far beyond our individual notes. Remember that you are never alone on this journey; countless others believe in you and your potential.

Girls, you are the architects of a future of compassion, innovation and limitless possibility. Believe in yourself, love yourself, and let your light shine brightly because the world is a better place with you in it.

Dream big, reach for the stars, and never forget that you can do anything you set your mind to. The world is waiting for the incredible impact that only you can make.

With love and unwavering belief in you,

....
[your name].

On her journey, she encountered many challenges. She had to trudge along thorny jungle paths, leap over rushing rivers, and crawl through dark caves. But with each step, her determination to find the flower grew stronger.

One night, as the forest was lit by a twinkling starry sky, Lila heard a faint song. She followed the sound, which led her to a clearing where, amidst a magnificent display of flowers, a beautiful flower bloomed. Its bright petals shimmered in a kaleidoscope of color, and a delicate scent filled the air.

Lila approached the flower slowly. She cautiously reached out and touched the flower, and a warm sensation flooded her body. Suddenly she felt the weight in her heart lift, as if the flower had dispelled her sadness and breathed love and hope into her.

The beautiful flower whispered softly to her: "There is immeasurable power within you. True beauty is not in the absence of sadness, but in dealing with it. Your heart is precious and you can light up the world with it.

Lila realized that her true strength was within. She returned to her village with a beautiful flower in her heart, bringing healing not only to herself but also to those who loved her. Her journey taught her that inner strength and self-acceptance are the keys to a fulfilled life. From that day on, Lila lived with an unwavering inner strength that never left her.

Story 2:
The Star Flight.

In the small town of Lumina lived Alice. She was fascinated by the twinkling stars. She dreamed of traveling through galaxies, gliding on starbeams, and being close to distant worlds. But in Alice's mind, the idea of touching the stars was just a dream - until the day she discovered an ancient book in the library.

The book, titled "The Art of Stellar Flight," revealed the secret of navigating the universe by starlight.

Alice was fascinated by the yellowed pages and ancient drawings that showed how to reach the stars. She decided that she would be the one to revive this ancient art.

Alice began her journey by studying star patterns and looking for patterns in the night sky. She spent many hours on a hill with her head in the clouds watching the stars move. Her determination to fly around the galaxy grew with each star she studied.

Eventually, Alice was able to use ancient methods of flight. She collected stardust in a small pouch to fuel her journey. Then, on a bright starry evening, she stepped out into the darkness to begin her journey.

Amid swirls of stellar light and webs of shooting stars, Alice traveled through the universe. She saw planets in bright colors, stars shining in fantastic formations, and galaxies performing an endless dance. The cosmic wind blew through her hair, and she felt freer than ever.

During her journey, Alice met strange beings - beings of light who lived in the depths of space. They shared with her stories and wisdom about the mysteries of the universe. Alice learned that the diversity of the world beyond Earth was as breathtaking as the stars she so admired.

When she finally returned to Earth, Alice was not the same girl. She realized that the world was much larger than she had ever imagined. But she also realized that her dreams were not out of reach - they were just a star flight away.

From that day on, Alice shone with the knowledge that with confidence, determination, and faith, one can reach the stars, and that the wonders of the universe are within reach of anyone who believes.

Story 3:
Song of the Ocean

In the depths of the sea, where corals glittered and fish swam in bright colors, there lived a little sea princess named Amara. She was different from other sea creatures - she had a special gift: her voice had the power to affect the balance of the ocean.

Amara loved to discover the secrets of the sea, but she was afraid of her own power. Her voice was so powerful that she feared it would upset the balance of the ocean. For fear of causing harm, she suppressed her voice and avoided singing.

One day, Amara found a sunken cave full of shiny shells and glowing seaweed. Inside the cave, she met an ancient turtle named Océane, who had once been a guardian of the sea. Océane saw Amara's potential and encouraged her to embrace her gift rather than fear it.

Under Océane's guidance, Amara began to sing. The melody that flowed from her heart was as gentle as an ocean breeze and as powerful as a mighty river. Her singing reached every corner of the ocean, soothing the rough waves and bringing harmony to the marine world.

As Amara learned to accept and embrace her voice, she discovered that she could keep the ocean in balance. She helped lost creatures, found lost treasures, and helped heal the sea.

But soon the sea was threatened by a violent storm that threatened to engulf everything. Amara realized that only she could restore the balance. With her singing, she calmed the troubled waves, drove away the storm, and restored calm to the sea.

Amara learned that her gift must be used responsibly. With confidence and respect for her abilities, she lived as a protector of the sea. She continued to sing her song of peace and harmony and became a legend, preserving the beauty and power of the sea. Her song reminded everyone that true strength lies not only in power, but in the wisdom to use it.

Story 4:
The butterfly garden

In a secluded part of the forest there was a secret garden that only the bravest could enter. There lived little Olive, a girl who loved the diversity of nature. But she often felt invisible, like a shadow in a colorful world.

One day, Olive heard about a magical place where butterflies fluttered in the most beautiful colors and shapes. She decided to visit this garden to find out what made it so special.

On her journey through the dense forest and gentle streams, she encountered many obstacles. But Olive's determination to find the butterfly garden was fueled by her love of nature and her longing for color and beauty.

She finally reached the clearing where the garden was hidden. There, butterflies fluttered in amazing patterns and colors. They moved through the air like dancing petals, bringing a smile to Olive's face.

But something in particular caught Olive's attention: Of all the butterflies, not one was the same color or shape. Some were tiny, some were large, some shimmered with the colors of the rainbow, some were as delicate as morning dew. Each one was as unique as Olive herself.

As she walked through the garden, she noticed that the butterflies gathered around her in a huge, colorful circle. She sensed that something magical was happening - they began to whisper that each girl was like a butterfly: unique and beautiful in her own way.

Olive realized that the beauty of diversity lies in individuality. She learned that even though she sometimes felt invisible, her uniqueness and individuality made her as beautiful as the butterflies around her.

With this realization, Olive returned to her village. She brought with her not only an awareness of the beauty of diversity, but also the conviction that each person is as unique as the butterfly in the garden. From that day on, Olive lived proudly as a girl who recognized that diversity and individuality are true treasures to be celebrated.

Story 5:
Flight of the Phoenix.

In a world where legends and magic collide, young Emilia lived. Her heart was full of dreams and hopes, until one day she was shaken by a great failure. Emilia felt as if an invisible darkness had enveloped her heart.

In the midst of this darkness, a radiant phoenix appeared, its wings shining brighter than the sun. The phoenix spoke softly to Emilia, inviting her to travel on its back and rise from its depths.

Emilia, overwhelmed by a spark of hope, agreed and mounted the majestic bird.

The phoenix flew high into the sky, through the clouds, the sun and the stars. Emilia felt the darkness slowly recede and her heart began to beat faster.

During the flight, the phoenix took Emilia to places where she could overcome her fears and insecurities. She encountered obstacles to overcome and trials to test her faith and determination.

Eventually, they reached the top of a mountain that overlooked the entire country. The Phoenix showed Emilia that the true value of escape is not in the destination, but in the journey itself. The ability to rise in the face of darkness and defeat was one of the greatest strengths one could possess.

With renewed courage, Emilia returned to her world on the back of a phoenix. She realized that it was not her failure that defined her, but her ability to learn from it and grow stronger.

Emilia began to share her experiences and became a source of inspiration for others who felt lost in the darkness. She taught that the phoenix fire is not only a symbol of rebirth, but also an inner drive that allows us to rise from the ashes of our failures and shine again.

From that day on, Emilia lived as a person who understood the power of rebirth and the strength that comes from overcoming difficulties. The flight of the phoenix was not only a journey of the body, but more importantly, a journey of the soul, which helped her to recognize and accept her own inner strength.

Story 6:
The Sound of
Friendship.

In a picturesque village on the edge of the forest lived a girl named Mia. Mia was known for her love of music. She had a special gift - she could hear the sounds of the world around her that were hidden from most people.

Mia listened to the melody of the wind, the rhythm of the streams, and the singing of the birds. But most of all, she loved the sound of people laughing. She believed that laughter was the most beautiful and joyful melody of all.

One day, as Mia walked through the woods, she heard a sad, soft sob.

She followed the sound and discovered a young owl trapped in a cave. The owl told Mia that it could no longer hear the melody of the forest because it was trapped.

Mia felt sorry for the owl and promised to help it. She sang a soft, soothing song and freed the owl. When the owl was finally free, it began to laugh - a bright, joyful laugh that filled the entire forest. Trees, flowers, and animals seemed to join in the laughter.

Mia realized that her gift of hearing the sounds of the world was not only for experiencing the joy of nature, but also for giving joy to others. She decided to help people find their own melodies of friendship.

Mia began composing songs that touched people's hearts. Her melodies encouraged people to find each other, make friends and share the joy of life. She started a music group in the village where people of all ages and backgrounds came together to sing and laugh.

Over time, the village became a place where friendship and happiness blossomed. Mia's songs brought people together and laughter became their constant companion. Mia understood that true friendship is the most beautiful melody of all.

Her message of friendship spread far beyond the village. People came from far away to listen to Mia and her music. They understood that true friendship and the sound of laughter make life richer and more beautiful.

Mia taught that the melodies of friendship and togetherness are stronger than all obstacles and differences. She showed that people can be connected through the power of music and laughter, regardless of their backgrounds.

From that day forward, Mia lived as a guardian of the melodies of friendship. She reminded the world that the sound of laughter is the most beautiful and powerful melody of all, and that true friendship has the power to connect hearts and fill lives with joy.

Story 7:
The Magic of Smiling.

In a small village of fragrant gardens and busy streets lived shy Sophia. She was a reserved girl with sparkling eyes and a smile that rarely visited her face. Sophia often felt invisible and thought she had little to offer.

One day, while walking in the woods, she met an old woman known as a storyteller. The wise woman noticed Sophia's quiet nature and told her an old legend about the magic of a smile.

The legend said that a unique smile had the power to bring joy and happiness to people's hearts. The wise woman saw the potential in Sophia and encouraged her to share her smile and bring joy to others.

Sophia was unsure at first, but decided to trust the old woman and embarked on a journey to discover the power of her smile.

Along the way, Sophia met people with very different stories and life experiences. She met children who shared their dreams, seniors who talked about times past, and people who struggled with challenges.

Sophia began to realize the magic of her smile. Her gentle smile could warm people's hearts. Children smiled when she told them their dreams, the elderly felt honored by her kindness and attention, and people with problems found comfort and hope in her smile.

As she traveled, Sophia felt her own heart fill with joy and happiness. The feedback and joy of the people around her made her realize that there was real magic in her smile.

During her journey, Sophia learned that self-love is the key to happiness. She realized that her smile not only brought joy to others, but also to herself. By giving love and joy to others, she found deep satisfaction within herself.

When Sophia returned to her village, she took the lessons of her journey with her. She smiled not only at others, but also at herself. Her smile became a symbol of joy and inner strength, encouraging others to accept themselves and find love in their hearts.

Sophia's story spread throughout the village and beyond. She became an ambassador for the magic of a smile, teaching people that true happiness lies not only in giving to others, but also in accepting and loving oneself. Her smile reminded everyone that within everyone's shyness and reserve lies a wonderful magic that can spread joy and happiness.

Story 8:
Anna and the Shadow Dance

Anna was a funny, creative girl. She had long blonde hair and an incredible passion for singing and dancing. She loved spending time in her little room, singing songs and dancing to her own music. But sometimes when she went outside, she would see other people doing things that seemed more interesting, and she began to feel that she was different.

One day, her friend Eliza told her about a secret dance school where children learned shadow dance.

This sparked Anna's interest. She imagined shadows following her to the rhythm of the music. She wanted to see how it was done!

When she arrived at the school, she saw an unusual phenomenon. The shadows the children were dancing with were moving to the rhythm of the music like little ballerinas. At first she was surprised, but when she saw the children dancing with the shadows, she realized that it wasn't just dancing, but something more.

The teacher explained to them that dancing with shadows helps them understand themselves and accept their differences.

This really moved Anna. All of these children, each with their own style of dance, had learned to accept and be proud of their shadows. Anna began to dance with her own shadow, discovering something new with each movement.

Her shadow changed shape, pirouetted, and seemed to glow like a rainbow. This made Anna realize that her difference was something beautiful, just like the colorful movements of her shadow when she danced.

When she returned home, she remembered all the magical moments at school. She told her family about her shadow dance. She also decided to tell her friends. She told them that the differences were cool and that their own shadows could be just as beautiful and impressive as those in dance school. She encouraged them to look at their shadows with pride and joy because that is what makes them so unique and beautiful.

Anna's story showed the girls that everyone is unique. She taught them that differences are wonderful and that they should be comfortable in their own skin. Because of her, the girls began to see their own shadows in a whole new light.

Story 9:
Clare, the Star Warrior

Once upon a time, in a small village surrounded by twinkling stars, there lived a girl named Clara. Clara was different from the others. She was brave and had a big dream - to become a star warrior and fight the darkness.

Clare believed that she could be a light in the darkness, but fears and insecurities held her back. Sometimes she felt she wasn't strong enough to make her dreams come true. But one night, as she stood under a clear starry sky, a warming ray of stardust enveloped her. This magical stardust gave Clara courage and strength.

Driven by her desire to become a star warrior, Clare embarked on a journey into the heart of darkness, where she faced her own fears and insecurities.

She encountered darkness in many forms - fear of failure, self-doubt, and the uncertainty that she wasn't good enough.

But with each step into the darkness, the stardust in her heart grew. The stardust around her began to glow, reminding her that she was special and strong.

Clare began to realize that it was okay to be afraid. She learned that it's not about not having fears, it's about accepting them and facing them. By facing her fears, she discovered a strength that lay deep within her - the strength to believe in herself.

Clare returned to her village with a heart full of stardust and new courage. She told the other girls about her journey and encouraged them to believe in themselves and overcome their own fears. She told them that everyone has a unique strength and that it is important to believe in it.

Clare's story became a legend in the village. She became known as a star warrior who found her own light in the darkness and showed others how to face their fears in order to grow and gain strength.

Clare's story taught the girls that it's okay to have fears and insecurities. She showed them that it's okay to believe in themselves and embrace their uniqueness, because that's what makes us strong and great.

Story: 10
The Mystery of the Labyrinth.

Isabell was a bright girl who lived in a small town near an enchanted forest. One day she heard of a mysterious maze that was said to be full of wonders and lessons in patience, perseverance, and trust.

Filled with curiosity and determination, Isabell set out to find the maze. She knew it would not be an easy task, but she felt drawn to this mysterious place.

The labyrinth was a true wonder, its high walls decorated with vines and flowers. Isabell entered it with a pounding heart and a desire to discover its secrets. But she soon realized that the path was not easy. The path was winding and it seemed that each step led further into the maze with no clear direction.

Isabell had learned that patience was the key to understanding the wonders of the labyrinth. She had to stay calm and walk slowly so as not to get lost. With each fork she passed, with each detour and dead end, she realized that the labyrinth was not just a physical place, but a journey into herself.

It was not just a path, but a test of her endurance. Isabell had to persevere, even though the path was long and arduous. She realized that each step was a part of her journey - a step that brought her closer to her own growth and strength.

As she walked through the maze, she realized that self-confidence was a prerequisite for moving forward. She had to rely on her skills, intuition, and knowledge to find the right path.

After a long and arduous journey through the maze, Isabell finally reached the heart of the puzzle.

There she found a small spring in which she could see her own reflection. She realized that the real secret of the maze lay within herself.

It was a journey that taught her patience with herself, perseverance in difficult moments, and faith in her own abilities. Isabell found her inner strength and realized that she was capable of overcoming obstacles and walking difficult paths.

With a clear mind and a strengthened heart, Isabell left the maze and returned to her small town. She told the other girls about her journey and taught them that life's true treasures are within. She encouraged them to trust their own abilities and believe in their own strengths, which would lead them on their own path through the maze of life.

Story 11:
Treasure of Time.

Sofia was a curious and adventurous young explorer. She lived in a picturesque village surrounded by green hills and clear lakes. One day she heard an old legend telling of a treasure - the most precious treasure of all, the Treasure of Time.

Sofia felt her excitement grow. She decided to go in search of this treasure, not knowing where she would find it, but determined to solve the mystery of time.

Her journey took her through dense forests, rugged mountains and along flowing rivers. Along the way, she met friendly creatures who helped and encouraged her. But the search for the treasure was not easy. She crossed difficult paths where she encountered obstacles. Time seemed to pass both quickly and slowly.

Sofia realized that time was the most precious gift she had. Every second that passed was irreversible and precious. She began to realize that it was not about finding the treasure at the end of the road, but rather about appreciating the value and importance of every second of life.

As she traveled, she learned to appreciate the moment. She savored the scent of flowers, the sound of the wind, and the smiles of the people she met. She saw the beauty in the little things that surrounded her and realized that the time she spent was precious.

It wasn't the treasure at the end of the journey that made it worthwhile, but the experiences she had along the way. Sofia found friendship, determination, and an appreciation for the present moment.

When she finally reached the place where the treasure of time was supposed to be, she stood in front of an old mirror that showed her own reflection. In that mirror she saw an echo of her journey, the realization that every moment is precious and that the true beauty of life is living in the moment.

Sofia returned to her village with a heart full of gratitude and wisdom. She told the other girls about her journey and taught them that the true treasure is not on the outside, but on the inside. She encouraged them to live in the moment, to find joy in the little things, and to cherish the time they have because that is the true treasure of life.

Chapter 12:
Melody of nature

Lena was a happy and adventurous girl who lived in a picturesque town surrounded by green hills and lush forests. One day she heard about a mysterious place in the deep forest where the melody of nature could be heard. The legend spoke of an enchanted place where the trees seemed to whisper and the birds sang a special song.

Full of curiosity and with a heart that strives for harmony, Lena set out to find this mysterious place. She knew it wouldn't be easy, but the idea of hearing the melody of nature fascinated her.

After carefully preparing for the journey, Lena entered the forest. She followed a path lined with moss-covered stones, and sunlight streamed through the treetops.

Eventually, Lena came to a clearing. The forest opened up into a beautiful place, surrounded by tall trees and a gently babbling brook. There was a unique harmony in the air. Birds were singing a soft song, accompanied by the rustling of leaves in the wind. It was as if nature itself was playing a melody that touched her soul.

Lena sat by the brook and listened to the melody of nature. With her eyes closed, she absorbed every sound, every breeze, every rustling of the leaves, and every bird song. She felt her own energy seem to merge with the energy of nature.

The sounds of nature began to play their own music in her heart, bringing strength and peace

As Lena absorbed the sounds of nature, she began to realize that her own inner harmony was closely connected to the harmony of nature. She realized that the sense of peace and tranquility she felt at that moment was a reflection of the harmony she found within herself.

When she finally stood up, she felt refreshed and fulfilled. She carried the harmony of nature in her heart and knew that she would always carry this melody of nature with her.

When Lena returned to the city, she told the other girls about her experience. She explained to them the importance of being in tune with nature in order to find their own inner harmony. She encouraged them to notice and appreciate the beauty and melody of nature in every moment, for in this connection lies the true strength and meaning of life.

Story: 13
Lucy and the rainbow catcher

Lucy lived in a world surrounded by gray. People went about their daily tasks and seemed to have forgotten what it was like to have joy and color in their lives. Lucy, a curious and vibrant little girl, felt crushed by the gloom surrounding her.

One day, as Lucy walked her dog in the park, a rainbow appeared in her eyes after a light drizzle.

This moment of color in the midst of the gray made her heart beat faster. This brief appearance of the rainbow gave her a sense of hope.

From that moment on, Lucy decided to become a rainbow catcher. She believed that she could not only catch rainbows, but also bring joy and color to the world. She began to observe her surroundings more carefully, looking for small, colorful things that could bring joy to others.

Lucy began to paint colorful pictures and put them up around town. She gave colorful flowers to people, smiled at strangers, and painted colorful rocks to scatter everywhere. She felt the gray slowly flood with color, and people began to see the beauty of simple, colorful gestures.

Her actions inspired others, and gradually people began to enjoy the small pleasures of life. The streets suddenly became colorful, and people began to smile and enjoy the small pleasures of everyday life.

The world, once filled with gloom, began to come alive. People saw joy in the little things and began to realize the power of color and the magic of life.

With her belief in color, Lucy changed the world in a new way. She captured the rainbow and brought it to life in a different way. Her belief in the power of color and joy made the world more vibrant and happier. She realized that finding joy in the little things makes life more colorful and beautiful.

Story: 14
Flight of the imagination.

Julia was a bright and imaginative girl who lived in a picturesque village surrounded by lush meadows and high mountains. She was a dreamer, lost in her thoughts and creativity. One day, while playing in a hidden clearing, she saw a mysterious book about dragons.

Inside, she found a legend about the connection between dragons and the power of imagination. The legend said that a world of fantasy could be discovered on the back of a dragon. Julia could not suppress her desire to explore this world. She dreamed of flying on a dragon's back and experiencing the wonders of fantasy.

One sunny day, while Julia was working on a particularly creative project, she heard a faint rustling in her garden. When she went outside, she discovered a magnificent, majestic dragon landing gently on the grass. With big, friendly eyes, he looked at Julia as if waiting for her.

Filled with awe and excitement, Julia realized that her dream had come true. The dragon invited her to climb onto his back. Without hesitation, Julia climbed onto the dragon as it soared majestically into the sky.

Together they flew above the village to a world that captured her imagination. They discovered a land where trees looked like giant butterflies and clouds floated in the sky like fluffy pillows. Colors exploded in an endless palette, and the air was filled with the most wonderful smells.

Julia began to explore the many facets of her imagination. The dragon took her to magical islands where she told stories, to fairy forests where she listened to music, and to sparkling lakes where she reflected her own dreams.

As she traveled on the dragon's back, Julia realized the power of her imagination. She realized that there was infinite creativity and power in her imagination. She learned that her imagination was a source of inspiration and freedom.

When Julia finally returned to her village, her heart was full of gratitude and excitement. She told the other girls about her amazing journey. She encouraged them to believe in their dreams and to trust their imaginations. Julia taught them that in the imagination lies a world of adventure, lessons, and inspiration, and that by believing in their own creativity, they can discover the meaning of self-love, friendship, and inner strength.

Stoty: 15
Crystal Spring

In a sleepy village called Avelore, there lived a girl named Isabella. Her heart was as vibrant as the colors of the rainbow. One day, Isabella heard of a mysterious place known as the Crystal Spring. Rumors circulated that the place reflected people's dreams and deepest desires.

Driven by curiosity, Isabella set out to find this mystical place. She followed a path of adventure and discovery through lush forests and bubbling streams until she finally discovered a clear, mysterious spring. It seemed to glow with the brightest colors, and shimmering crystals danced on the bottom.

She leaned over the spring and saw her own reflection. But instead of her normal reflection, she saw a multitude of sparkling crystals, refracted in different colors and patterns. Intrigued, she reached out her hand and the crystals formed around her palm, shimmering and sparkling.

At that moment, Isabella had a profound realization. She realized that the dreams in her heart were as precious and special as those sparkling crystals. Her dreams were the essence of herself, a reflection of her own personality and individuality.

The Crystal Spring took Isabella on a journey that reflected her thoughts and desires. Each of her dreams, each of her innermost hopes, was manifested in the sparkling crystals. Isabella realized that she was the creator of her own reality, that her dreams reflected the beauty and uniqueness of her soul.

With this new understanding, Isabella returned to her village. She told the other girls about her adventure at the Crystal Spring and encouraged them to believe in the importance of their own dreams and desires. Isabella taught them that dreams are the essence of their unique personalities and that they have the power to shape their reality.

The girls at Avelore began to believe in their own dreams and realized that they were the source of their strength and uniqueness. They learned that self-love, friendship, and inner strength are closely related to valuing their own dreams. In this way, Isabella's legacy lives on as an inspiration for girls to cherish and achieve their dreams.

Chapter 16: Dream circus, Vanessa's trial of courage.

Once upon a time there lived a cheerful girl named Vanessa who had a big dream: she wanted to become a circus artist. From acrobatics and juggling to daring stunts on a tightrope, Vanessa could imagine nothing better than delighting audiences with her art. However, there was one problem that slowed her down - a fear of heights.

Every day Vanessa watched with fascination the breathtaking performances of the small circus in her town. She admired the skill of the performers as they whirled effortlessly through the air. But every time she thought about floating high in the circus dome, it made her sick.

One day Vanessa decided it was time to overcome her fears. She talked to her circus friends, clowns, trapeze artists and jugglers, about her dream and challenge. To her surprise, they all immediately wanted to help her.

Together they started with small steps. First Vanessa stood on a low platform, and then she dared to enter the trapeze.

Her new friends were always by her side, encouraging and supporting her. Vanessa realized that she was not alone in the circus community.

The clowns made her laugh when fear threatened to overwhelm her. The trapeze artists showed her how to control her body and turn heights into a kind of dance. The jugglers taught her to focus on balance and get rid of her fears.

Over time, Vanessa's skills not only grew, but so did her inner strength. She realized that the support of her circus friends was invaluable not only for her dreams, but also for her personal development.

Finally, the day of the big performance arrived. Vanessa stood high on the trapeze, the audience below her and felt the wind in her face.

Fear still lingered in her, but she had learned to control it. She performed her tricks with a smile and received thunderous applause.

Vanessa not only overcame her fear of heights, but also discovered the true meaning of teamwork and friendship. The audience learned from her story that dreams are not always easy to achieve, but with determination, support and a strong belief in yourself, they can come true. In this way, the Circus of Dreams became not only a place of magic and entertainment, but also a source of inspiration for young girls who want to pursue their own dreams.

Chapter 17: Agnes, the brave explorer.

Agnes, a happy little girl with wild curls and bright eyes, lived in a quiet village surrounded by green meadows and friendly neighbors. But Agnes dreamed of more - of faraway lands, unknown adventures, and mysteries to be discovered.

One day, Agnes came upon an abandoned house at the edge of the village. It had an aura of mystery about it, and most children avoided it for fear of ghost stories. But Agnes felt a strange attraction and couldn't resist. With her heart pounding, she entered the old building.

Inside, Agnes discovered dusty furniture, broken glass in the windows, and a weathered fireplace.

But what caught her attention the most was a yellowed diary on a dusty desk. Agnes carefully opened it and began to read the entries.

The words transported her to the world of an intrepid adventurer named Amelia, who traveled through unknown lands many years ago. Amelia tamed wild animals, discovered exotic plants, and met friendly tribes. Agnes was fascinated by the experiences she found in the yellowed pages.

Determined to embark on an adventure of her own, Agnes began packing provisions and drawing a map. Her parents were concerned when they learned of her plans, but they saw the determination in Agnes' eyes and finally gave in.

With diary in hand and a smile on her face, Agnes set out. She traveled through dense forests, crossed raging rivers, and climbed steep hills.

Along the way, she met friendly animals and discovered hidden places that no one in the village knew about.

During her journey, Agnes realized that the true discovery was not only in the outside world, but also in her own heart. She conquered her fears and gained courage and confidence. Each step on the unknown path helped her to understand herself better.

After many days, Agnes returned to her village full of stories and experiences.

The villagers were amazed at her adventurous spirit and admired her courage.

Agnes smiled, knowing that she had discovered not only the world around her, but also the treasure within herself - the strength to be brave and to live her own curiosity.

This story tells of Agnes' courageous journey to discover not only the mysteries of the world, but also her inner strength and determination. It is an encouragement to every young girl to follow her dreams and explore the world with a brave heart.

Story 18:
The Colorful Canvas of the Invisible Artist Ella

Ella loved to paint. She spent every spare moment with brush and paint, conjuring her thoughts and dreams onto canvas. But no one knew of her talent but herself. Fear of criticism and ridicule kept Ella from sharing her art with the world. Instead, she hid her masterpieces in a sketchbook known only to herself.

Then one day, the halls of her school echoed with the announcement of an art contest. Ella's heart began to beat faster. A mixture of excitement and uncertainty filled her as she read the announcement. "Why not?" she thought. With a deep breath, Ella overcame her fear and decided to share her art with the world.

The weeks that followed were filled with intense work and exhausting emotions. Ella painted with passion and dedication, pouring her thoughts and feelings into every brush stroke. When she finally submitted her work, she felt both liberated and vulnerable.

Time passed and the day of the jury's decision drew near. Ella could barely sleep, so plagued was she by doubt and uncertainty. But the day had come. The school eagerly gathered in the art room where the contestants' work was displayed.

As Ella's paintings were unveiled, the room was filled with a sense of awe. The colors danced vividly on the canvas and the judges gazed in awe at Ella's work. Her heart was beating so loud she thought the whole world could hear it.

To her surprise and delight, Ella not only won the art contest, but also received praise and recognition from her classmates. The invisible artist was no longer invisible. Her fear of criticism turned into a powerful courage that inspired not only herself, but others as well.

Ella became a symbol of courage for aspiring artists at her school. Her example showed the importance of overcoming fear and sharing one's talents with the world. The invisible artist's colorful canvas now glowed with the most beautiful colors, and Ella's story encouraged many little girls to follow their own paths with confidence and courage.

Dear Parents.

It is a good idea for girls to keep a "confidence journal," which can be a positive and empowering approach. In this journal, they can freely express their insecurities, fears, and anxieties as a way to externalize and process their feelings. Here are some examples of how these fears can be addressed or changed:

1. Fear of Failure
   - Write about a specific fear of failure.
   - Solution: Break down a big goal into smaller, achievable tasks. Celebrate small victories and understand that mistakes are a natural part of learning and growth.

2. Fear of rejection or criticism:
   - You are afraid of what others will think or say.
   - Solution: Focus on self-affirmation and self-love. Remember that everyone faces criticism and that it is an opportunity for growth. Surround yourself with supportive people.

3. Doubts about your abilities:
   - List doubts about your personal skills or talents.
   - Solution: Make a list of accomplishments and positive feedback you have received in the past. Recognize that you can improve with practice and that everyone has unique strengths.

4. Fear of the Unknown/Future:
   - Write about your uncertainty about the future.
   - Solution: Break down future goals into smaller, more manageable steps. Focus on the present and what you can do today. Go on a journey and realize that it's okay not to know everything.

5. - Don't compare yourself to others.
   - Comparing yourself to others makes you feel inadequate.
   - The solution: Celebrate your own journey and your own successes. Understand that everyone develops at their own pace. Use others as inspiration, not a measure of your own worth.

6. Fear of speaking up:
   - Write down fears about expressing opinions or ideas.
   - Solution: Practice speaking up in a safe environment, such as with friends or family. Realize that your voice is valuable and that sharing your thoughts contributes to personal growth and collective understanding.

7. Fear of not fitting in:
  - Identify your fear of social acceptance.
  - Solution: Embrace your individuality and uniqueness. Seek out peers and communities. Focus on the qualities that make you unique and build bonds based on shared interests.

Encouraging girls to recognize and reframe their insecurities helps build resilience and confidence. By adopting a positive attitude, they can face challenges with a sense of strength and confidence.

Keeping a confidence journal can be an effective tool for managing your emotions and increasing your sense of balance. Below is a sample entry that you can use as inspiration for writing down your thoughts and feelings. Remember, this is only a suggestion and your entries should be authentic and reflect your personal experience.

Believe in yourself.

Today I am starting a new chapter in my life, I have decided to focus on the positive and believe in myself. I am experiencing all kinds of emotions, but instead of focusing on what can go wrong, I want to pay attention to what is good and valuable.

Positive things I noticed today

1. Successes from the previous day: Today I remember all the accomplishments and small successes from yesterday. Even the smallest steps lead to progress.

2. Support from my loved ones: I realize that I have people around me who support and love me. This increases my sense of security.

3. My strong protectors: I think about what makes me strong. Is it my skills, my determination, or my inner strength? They are worth appreciating.

Negative aspects that scare me:

1. Fear of failure: Although I fear failure, I remind myself that it is a part of life and an opportunity to learn and grow.

2. Low self-esteem: Sometimes I feel that I am not good enough. Today I will think about what I can do to increase my self-confidence.

3. Uncertainty about the future: Instead of worrying about what will happen tomorrow, I will focus on what I can do today to shape my future.

This journal will help you focus on the positive aspects of life and gain confidence. I hope that through daily reflection, I will become more aware of my strengths and be able to face difficulties with more optimism.

Confidence Journal.

Write down both good and bad things that scare you.
Get rid of bad feelings

Confidence Journal.

Write down both good and bad things that scare you.
Get rid of bad feelings

Confidence Journal.

Write down both good and bad things that scare you.
Get rid of bad feelings

We create our books with love
and great care.
Your feedback will help us
improve this book and create
new ones.
Your opinion matters a lot.
Support us and leave a review.

Thanks for your purchase

Bonus:
Download Free
e-book
Riddles, and
Trivia for Smart
Kids